UNDERSTAND GEOGRAPHY OF THE EUROPE

IMPORTANT FOR UPSC AND OTHER STATE PCS EXAMINATION.

K.BASU

To the Readers and Aspirants

Contents

CHAPTER ONE

EUROPE-I

ABOUT EUROPE:

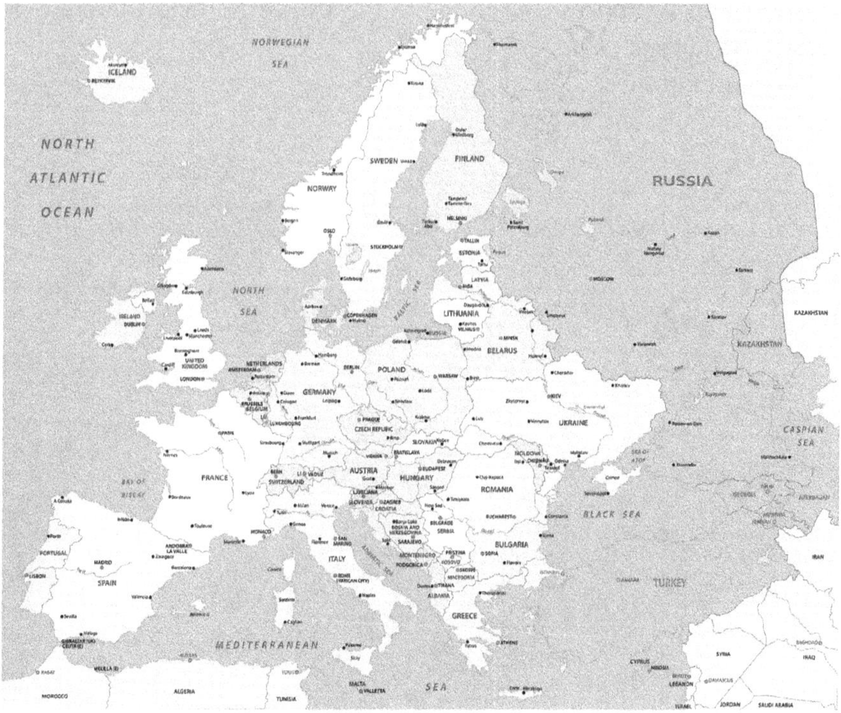

Political Map of Europe

- Europe is the **second-smallest** continent in the World that occupying the western portion of the Eurasian landmass.
- Europe is a continent located entirely in the Northern Hemisphere and mostly in the Eastern Hemisphere.
- Europe is also described as a **"peninsula of peninsulas"** and and the 'Peninsula of Eurasia'.
- Eurasia is the name given to the combined land area of Europe and Asia.
- Europe comprises of 10% of the world's population.

Europe has divided the continent into different regions:

There are ten countries in Northern Europe, ten in Eastern Europe, nine in Western Europe, and fifteen in Southern Europe.

Number of Countries: According to the United Nations, there are 44 countries in Europe.

Northern Europe:

Map-I

- Northern Europe is made up of ten sovereign nations. These ten countries are Denmark, Estonia, Finland, Iceland, Ireland, Latvia, Lithuania, Norway, Sweden, and United Kingdom.
- Countries like Lithuania, Latvia, and Estonia form a part of the **Baltic region**; the United Kingdom and Ireland form a part of the British Isles; and the remaining countries like Finland, Iceland, Norway, Denmark and Sweden form a part of **Scandinavia**.
- The United Kingdom is most populous nation and Iceland is least populous nation in Europe.

Eastern Europe:

Map-II

- There are Ten sovereign nations such as Belarus, Bulgaria, Czechia, Hungary, Poland, the Republic of Moldova, Romania, the Russian Federation, Slovakia, and Ukraine.
- Russia is the biggest and most populous nation in all of Europe.

Western Europe:

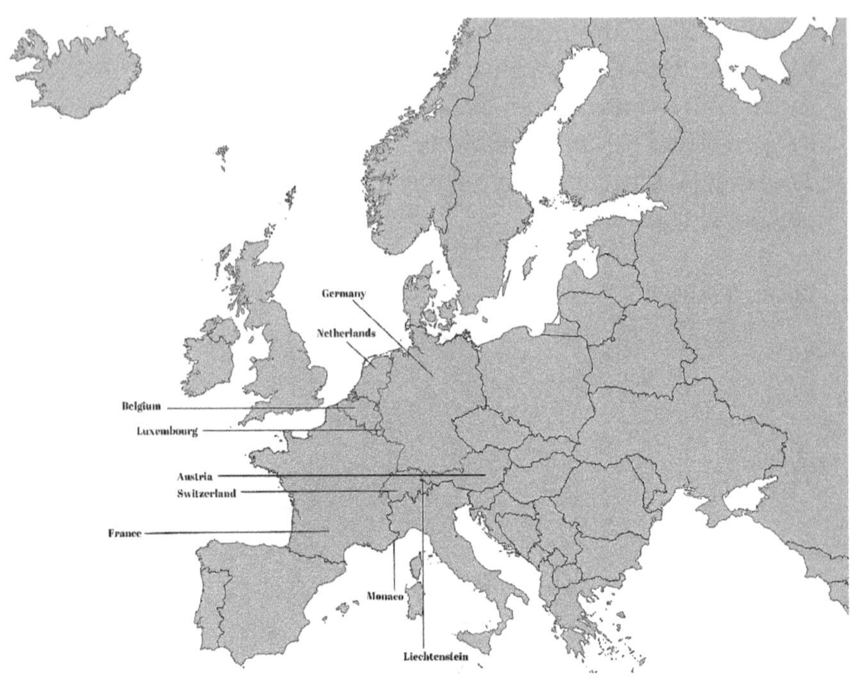

Map-III

- Western Europe is made up of nine sovereign nations.
- Such as Austria, Belgium, France, Germany, Liechtenstein, Luxembourg, Monaco, Netherlands, and Switzerland.
- Western Europe is also one of the world's richest regions and European continent's biggest cities like Paris, Berlin, Vienna, Hamburg, Marseille, Zurich etc are situated.
- Germany is Western Europe's most populous country and Europe's second-most populous country.

- Germany is Europe's highest GDP and the biggest financial surplus of any country.

Southern Europe:

Map-IV

- Southern Europe is also known as Mediterranean Europe.
- It comprises of fifteen sovereign Albania, Andorra, Bosnia and Herzegovina, Croatia,Greece, Italy, Malta, Montenegro, North Macedonia, Portugal, San Marino, Serbia, Slovenia, Spain, and Vatican City.
- Italy is Southern Europe's most populous country.

Transcontinental Countries:

Transcontinental countries are nations that have territories on two continents, in this case, both Asia and Europe. **Russia, Turkey, Kazakhstan, Azerbaijan, Georgia, Armenia, and Cyprus** are some of the ranscontinental countries.-**Important for UPSC Prelims and State PSC Exam.**

UNDERSTAND GEOGRAPHY OF THE EUROPE

CHAPTER TWO

EUROPE-II

ABOUT PHYSICAL EUROPE:

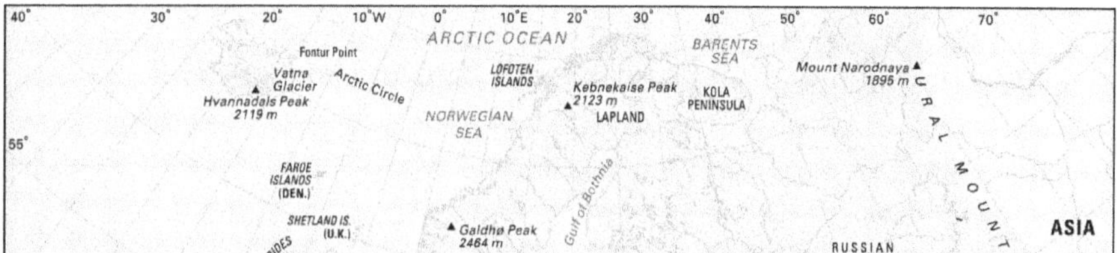

Map

- It is surrounded by water-bodies in three sides- Arctic Ocean in the north, Atlantic Ocean in the west, and Mediterranean Sea in the south.
- It is separated from Asia by Caspian Sea and Ural mountains.

- Finland is called the **'Land of Lakes'** because several lakes are formed due to the melting of ice-sheets.
- Spain and Portugal together form the **'Iberia'.**
- Yugoslavia, Greece, Romania and Albania, situated on the coast of Black Sea and Mediterranean Sea are called **'Balkan states'.**
- Lithuania, Latvia and Estonia are together called **'Baltic states'.**
- **Major Mountain Ranges:** Cantabrian, Pyrenees, Apennines, Dinaric **Alps,** Carpathian, Kjolen and Balkan ranges.
- **Mt. Elbrus** is the highest peak of Europe.
- **Major Rivers:** Danube, Dnieper, Don, Elbe, Loire, Oder, Po, Rhine, Rhone, Shannon, Tagus and Volga.
- **The Volga** is the longest river in the Europe,
- **Rhine River** is the busiest waterway of Europe.
- **Po River** is called the 'Ganges of Italy'.
- **Danube river** is the second longest river of Europe.
- Capital of Ukraine " **Kyiv**" situated near bank of **Dnieper River.**

CHAPTER THREE

EUROPE-III

ABOUT STRAITS IN EUROPE:

Strait is geographical region where thin channel of a waterway connects two large water bodies but separates two large landforms.

List of some important strait in Europe:

- **The Strait of Gibraltar:** connects North Atlantic ocean with Mediterranean sea but separate the Iberian Peninsula Spain in Europe from Morocco in Africa.
- **Kerch Strait:** connects sea of Azov with Black sea but separate Russia from Ukraine.
- **Bosporus Strait or Strait of Istanbul:** It is a narrowest strait in the world that connects Black sea with sea of Marmara but separate Europe from Asia.
- **Dardanelles or Strait of Gallipoli:** connects the Sea of Marmara with the Aegean sea.
- **Dover Strait:** connects English channel with North sea but separate U.K from France.
- **Denmark Strait:** connects Arctic Ocean with North Atlantic ocean.
- **North Channel:** connects the Irish Sea with the Atlantic Ocean.
- **Strait of Sicily:** It separate Sicily from Tunisia.

CHAPTER FOUR

EUROPE-IV

STATIC GK OF EUROPE:

- Steppe region of Ukraine is called the 'Granary of the world' or 'Bread Basket of the World.
- Milan is known as 'Manchester of Italy'.
- Moscow is called the 'Port of Five Seas' i.e Caspian Sea, Black Sea, Baltic Sea, White Sea and Lake Ladoga.
- International Seed bank is established in the Swelbard Island of Norway.
- Nord Stream is a network of offshore natural gas pipelines project under Baltic sea between Russia and Germany.
- **List of Mountain peak in descending orders:**
    Mount Elbrus (Russia) > Mont Blanc(France) >Mount Etna(Italy)
- Alps Mountain range is longest Mountain range in Europe.
- Black sea and Caspian sea connected by Mountain Caucasus in Russia.
- Caspian sea bordered by countries : Turkmenistan, Kazakhstan, Russia,Azerbaijan and Iran.
- Black sea bordered by countries: Turkey,Georgia,Russia,Ukraine,Romania and Bulgaria.
- The Caspian Sea is the world's largest inland body of water and the world's largest lake.
- Mount Stromboli is Volcanic Mountain in Sicily also known as "Lighthouse of the Mediterranean".

CHAPTER FIVE

Special chapter: Russia

ABOUT RUSSIA:

Map-I

- Russia is world's largest country in total area and a wide diversity of landforms.
- The central and southern areas of Russia include large fertile areas, marsh, steppes (plains without trees).
- Siberia is a combination of frozen tundra, with rolling hills rising to plateaus.
- The country's highest point is Mt. Elbrus.
- Some of the world's longest rivers such as Volga, Dnieper and Dvina (west), the Lena, Ob, and Yenisey (central) and the Amur.

- Lake Baikal is the deepest and among the clearest of all lakes in the World.
- Russia contains the world's largest reserve of coniferous wood.
- Lena river is longest river of Russia.

Political system:

Map-II

- Russia has 46 provinces: 21 republics,4 autonomous,9 krays,2 federal cities and 1 autonomous.
- Moscow is federal city and capital city of Russia.

Location Map of Russia:

Map-III

- Russia is world's largest country by area, stretches from Northern Asia to Eastern Europe.
- Russia Bordered by Georgia, Kazakhstan, Ukraine, Estonia, Finland, Belarus, Lithuania, Latvia, Poland, Azerbaijan, North Korea, China.

CHAPTER SIX

Special chapter: Ukraine

• 14 •

ABOUT UKRAINE:

Map-I

- Ukraine is the largest country that is entirely within Europe.
- The country's highest point is Hoverla Mountain.
- Central Ukraine is covered by plateaus and fertile plains.
- The Dnieper River, one of the major rivers of Europe flows from Russia, through Belarus and Ukraine, to the Black Sea.

Provinces Of Ukraine Map:

Map-II

- Ukraine is divided into 24 provinces alongwith 1 autonomous,2 municipalities.
- Ukraine is the 2nd largest country by area in Europe.
- Kiev (Kyiv) – the capital and the most populous city of Ukraine.
- Kiev is the chief cultural and industrial center of Eastern Europe.

Location Map of Ukraine:

Map-III

- Ukraine is an Eastern European country.
- Ukraine is bordered by 7 European Nations such as Russia, Hungary, Romania, Moldova, Slovakia, Belarus, Poland.